Questions lovingly answered by:

_______________ & _______________

How do I love thee? Let me count the ways.
I love thee to the depth and breadth and height
My soul can reach, when feeling out of sight
For the ends of being and ideal grace.
I love thee to the level of every day's
Most quiet need, by sun and candle-light.
I love thee freely, as men strive for right.
I love thee purely, as they turn from praise.
I love thee with the passion put to use
In my old griefs, and with my childhood's faith.
I love thee with a love I seemed to lose
With my lost saints. I love thee with the breath,
Smiles, tears, of all my life; and, if God choose,
I shall but love thee better after death.

- Elizabeth Barrett Browning -

How do you think your life has been going this year?

☐ HER REPLY ☐ HIS REPLY

☐ HIS REPLY ☐ HER REPLY

What are the risks with your beliefs?

☐ HER REPLY ☐ HIS REPLY

☐ HIS REPLY ☐ HER REPLY

If you are going to use your power, will you try different things? Why?

☐ HER REPLY ☐ HIS REPLY   ☐ HIS REPLY ☐ HER REPLY

What have you learned from your mistakes?

☐ HER REPLY ☐ HIS REPLY   ☐ HIS REPLY ☐ HER REPLY

What's the best way to find out if you're not alone?

☐ HER REPLY ☐ HIS REPLY

☐ HIS REPLY ☐ HER REPLY

What is the worst part of being in high school?

☐ HER REPLY ☐ HIS REPLY

☐ HIS REPLY ☐ HER REPLY

How much parenting does the child need to talk about?

☐ HER REPLY ☐ HIS REPLY

☐ HIS REPLY ☐ HER REPLY

What first turns you on?

☐ HER REPLY ☐ HIS REPLY

☐ HIS REPLY ☐ HER REPLY

List of things that would end a game

☐ HER REPLY ☐ HIS REPLY

☐ HIS REPLY ☐ HER REPLY

Do you believe in the afterlife? Why? Why not?

☐ HER REPLY ☐ HIS REPLY

☐ HIS REPLY ☐ HER REPLY

How do you deal with things that could impede your plan?

☐ HER REPLY ☐ HIS REPLY

☐ HIS REPLY ☐ HER REPLY

If you could do one thing in your life over again, what would it be?

☐ HER REPLY ☐ HIS REPLY

☐ HIS REPLY ☐ HER REPLY

How would you describe the feeling of being in love with someone?

☐ HER REPLY ☐ HIS REPLY

☐ HIS REPLY ☐ HER REPLY

How would you describe the feeling of being missed?

☐ HER REPLY ☐ HIS REPLY

☐ HIS REPLY ☐ HER REPLY

How would you describe the feeling of being alone without the internet?

☐ HER REPLY ☐ HIS REPLY   ☐ HIS REPLY ☐ HER REPLY

What is the one thing that you would give to be like a superhero?

☐ HER REPLY ☐ HIS REPLY   ☐ HIS REPLY ☐ HER REPLY

Why is it that all the important things you have to do to have a pretty night out will ensure it is going to be horrible and a riot?

☐ HER REPLY ☐ HIS REPLY   ☐ HIS REPLY ☐ HER REPLY

She looked at him like there was something wrong on his face; like… [continue the sentence]

☐ HER REPLY ☐ HIS REPLY   ☐ HIS REPLY ☐ HER REPLY

What was the happiest moment in your life?

☐ HER REPLY ☐ HIS REPLY   ☐ HIS REPLY ☐ HER REPLY

Say something that makes them angry

☐ HER REPLY ☐ HIS REPLY   ☐ HIS REPLY ☐ HER REPLY

If you could travel, where would you go?

☐ HER REPLY ☐ HIS REPLY

☐ HIS REPLY ☐ HER REPLY

What did you do today that made you think you're awesome?

☐ HER REPLY ☐ HIS REPLY

☐ HIS REPLY ☐ HER REPLY

What is your favorite thing about your body?

☐ HER REPLY   ☐ HIS REPLY   ☐ HIS REPLY   ☐ HER REPLY

How do you make the most of your time?

☐ HER REPLY   ☐ HIS REPLY   ☐ HIS REPLY   ☐ HER REPLY

What if you could choose something that doesn't exist? What would you do?

☐ HER REPLY ☐ HIS REPLY

☐ HIS REPLY ☐ HER REPLY

How can you find out what are your greatest strengths?

☐ HER REPLY ☐ HIS REPLY

☐ HIS REPLY ☐ HER REPLY

What is the best thing you can do to reduce your dependency on foreign dependencies?

☐ HER REPLY ☐ HIS REPLY

☐ HIS REPLY ☐ HER REPLY

If you could be someone famous for one hour and it would change your life, who would you be?

☐ HER REPLY ☐ HIS REPLY

☐ HIS REPLY ☐ HER REPLY

Say something about your family.

☐ HER REPLY ☐ HIS REPLY

☐ HIS REPLY ☐ HER REPLY

If you could go back to just one moment in your past, what would it be and why?

☐ HER REPLY ☐ HIS REPLY

☐ HIS REPLY ☐ HER REPLY

What do you think your least strong point is?

☐ HER REPLY ☐ HIS REPLY

☐ HIS REPLY ☐ HER REPLY

What's the difference between being mad and being amused?

☐ HER REPLY ☐ HIS REPLY

☐ HIS REPLY ☐ HER REPLY

Do you have any funny stories you can share about someone you know?

☐ HER REPLY ☐ HIS REPLY

☐ HIS REPLY ☐ HER REPLY

List of things that I want to work on in the near future

☐ HER REPLY ☐ HIS REPLY

☐ HIS REPLY ☐ HER REPLY

What is one thing in this place that does not get changed?

☐ HER REPLY ☐ HIS REPLY

☐ HIS REPLY ☐ HER REPLY

How many books have you read?

☐ HER REPLY ☐ HIS REPLY

☐ HIS REPLY ☐ HER REPLY

If you had to choose only one video to share with your friends and family this week, what would it be?

☐ HER REPLY ☐ HIS REPLY

☐ HIS REPLY ☐ HER REPLY

Will you be willing to spend a great deal of time with others? To whom and why?

☐ HER REPLY ☐ HIS REPLY

☐ HIS REPLY ☐ HER REPLY

What do you first remember about you and your mother?

☐ HER REPLY ☐ HIS REPLY

☐ HIS REPLY ☐ HER REPLY

What is your favorite color?

☐ HER REPLY ☐ HIS REPLY

☐ HIS REPLY ☐ HER REPLY

What is most important to you and why?

☐ HER REPLY ☐ HIS REPLY

☐ HIS REPLY ☐ HER REPLY

Where would you spend all your time if you could?

☐ HER REPLY ☐ HIS REPLY

☐ HIS REPLY ☐ HER REPLY

What is the one thing you really have to come to terms with?

☐ HER REPLY   ☐ HIS REPLY

☐ HIS REPLY   ☐ HER REPLY

Do you like to do things that involve hard work?

☐ HER REPLY   ☐ HIS REPLY

☐ HIS REPLY   ☐ HER REPLY

What should you be thankful for?

☐ HER REPLY ☐ HIS REPLY ☐ HIS REPLY ☐ HER REPLY

What are your favorite books that you never read?

☐ HER REPLY ☐ HIS REPLY ☐ HIS REPLY ☐ HER REPLY

What is one thing you have in common with your favorite band?

☐ HER REPLY ☐ HIS REPLY

☐ HIS REPLY ☐ HER REPLY

How do you deal with the negative effects?

☐ HER REPLY ☐ HIS REPLY

☐ HIS REPLY ☐ HER REPLY

Did you ever have any "What if" stories? What are those?

☐ HER REPLY ☐ HIS REPLY

☐ HIS REPLY ☐ HER REPLY

What's the biggest lie you've ever told?

☐ HER REPLY ☐ HIS REPLY

☐ HIS REPLY ☐ HER REPLY

What's your favorite thing to do with your friends?

☐ HER REPLY ☐ HIS REPLY

☐ HIS REPLY ☐ HER REPLY

What do you think is the most important quality of a successful person?

☐ HER REPLY ☐ HIS REPLY

☐ HIS REPLY ☐ HER REPLY

What would you do if you're stuck in a relationship where you can't have it?

☐ HER REPLY ☐ HIS REPLY

☐ HIS REPLY ☐ HER REPLY

Do you want to talk about a certain topic?

☐ HER REPLY ☐ HIS REPLY

☐ HIS REPLY ☐ HER REPLY

If you could, what would you take with you?

☐ HER REPLY ☐ HIS REPLY   ☐ HIS REPLY ☐ HER REPLY

If you could have any animal on Earth, what would it be?

☐ HER REPLY ☐ HIS REPLY   ☐ HIS REPLY ☐ HER REPLY

List of things that will never get sorted

☐ HER REPLY ☐ HIS REPLY

☐ HIS REPLY ☐ HER REPLY

How can you teach your son to be good at something?

☐ HER REPLY ☐ HIS REPLY

☐ HIS REPLY ☐ HER REPLY

What is more important to you to honor those to whom you
owe the most?

☐ HER REPLY ☐ HIS REPLY   ☐ HIS REPLY ☐ HER REPLY

How does your own universe work?

☐ HER REPLY ☐ HIS REPLY   ☐ HIS REPLY ☐ HER REPLY

List of things that need to be fixed as you find them

☐ HER REPLY ☐ HIS REPLY

☐ HIS REPLY ☐ HER REPLY

What are you doing to make it happen?

☐ HER REPLY ☐ HIS REPLY

☐ HIS REPLY ☐ HER REPLY

How do you get out of the house and interact with other people?

☐ HER REPLY ☐ HIS REPLY

☐ HIS REPLY ☐ HER REPLY

What's your goal?

☐ HER REPLY ☐ HIS REPLY

☐ HIS REPLY ☐ HER REPLY

What's the weirdest thing you have ever eaten?

☐ HER REPLY ☐ HIS REPLY

____
____
____
____
____
____
____
____

☐ HIS REPLY ☐ HER REPLY

____
____
____
____
____
____
____
____

Tell about a time when you had to face one of your greatest fears.

☐ HER REPLY ☐ HIS REPLY

____
____
____
____
____
____
____
____

☐ HIS REPLY ☐ HER REPLY

____
____
____
____
____
____
____
____

If you had to pick one word to describe your first impression
of a country, what would it be?

☐ HER REPLY ☐ HIS REPLY   ☐ HIS REPLY ☐ HER REPLY

Are you feeling anything special when you play it? Why?

☐ HER REPLY ☐ HIS REPLY   ☐ HIS REPLY ☐ HER REPLY

What's the thing that makes you most want to be successful?

☐ HER REPLY ☐ HIS REPLY   ☐ HIS REPLY ☐ HER REPLY

What is one thing that a player can never grow out of?

☐ HER REPLY ☐ HIS REPLY   ☐ HIS REPLY ☐ HER REPLY

If you could spend eternity in the same room with an animal, what would you think?

☐ HER REPLY ☐ HIS REPLY   ☐ HIS REPLY ☐ HER REPLY

What do your children like to watch?

☐ HER REPLY ☐ HIS REPLY   ☐ HIS REPLY ☐ HER REPLY

What is the best party you have ever been to?

☐ HER REPLY ☐ HIS REPLY

☐ HIS REPLY ☐ HER REPLY

What is one book that is a must-read?

☐ HER REPLY ☐ HIS REPLY

☐ HIS REPLY ☐ HER REPLY

If you could go back in time to the day you were born, what would you want to do?

☐ HER REPLY   ☐ HIS REPLY   ☐ HIS REPLY   ☐ HER REPLY

What is wisdom and how does it come about?

☐ HER REPLY   ☐ HIS REPLY   ☐ HIS REPLY   ☐ HER REPLY

List of things that you didn't think was feasible, but did it

☐ HER REPLY ☐ HIS REPLY

☐ HIS REPLY ☐ HER REPLY

What can you do to help you be more open by helping others in your life?

☐ HER REPLY ☐ HIS REPLY

☐ HIS REPLY ☐ HER REPLY

List of things that I should exclude

☐ HER REPLY ☐ HIS REPLY

☐ HIS REPLY ☐ HER REPLY

Do you like people who understand what you feel? Why?

☐ HER REPLY ☐ HIS REPLY

☐ HIS REPLY ☐ HER REPLY

How are your mother and grandmother alike?

☐ HER REPLY ☐ HIS REPLY   ☐ HIS REPLY ☐ HER REPLY

What's your first reaction when you start to use your new powers?

☐ HER REPLY ☐ HIS REPLY   ☐ HIS REPLY ☐ HER REPLY

What do you drink after the workday?

☐ HER REPLY ☐ HIS REPLY

☐ HIS REPLY ☐ HER REPLY

What is the most difficult part of being a (insert your job)?

☐ HER REPLY ☐ HIS REPLY

☐ HIS REPLY ☐ HER REPLY

What is the one thing you wish someone had told you when you were a kid?

☐ HER REPLY ☐ HIS REPLY

☐ HIS REPLY ☐ HER REPLY

What would you tell someone on the street about what you believe?

☐ HER REPLY ☐ HIS REPLY

☐ HIS REPLY ☐ HER REPLY

List of things that need to be in a certain order in your head

☐ HER REPLY ☐ HIS REPLY

☐ HIS REPLY ☐ HER REPLY

How would you describe the feeling of being inside of a body for the first time?

☐ HER REPLY ☐ HIS REPLY

☐ HIS REPLY ☐ HER REPLY

Why do you think everyone else has these thoughts anyway?

☐ HER REPLY ☐ HIS REPLY   ☐ HIS REPLY ☐ HER REPLY

Did any ideas come to you that you could not afford to do at that time?

☐ HER REPLY ☐ HIS REPLY   ☐ HIS REPLY ☐ HER REPLY

What are you afraid of? Why?

☐ HER REPLY ☐ HIS REPLY   ☐ HIS REPLY ☐ HER REPLY

What's so horrible about the world that it isn't worth trying to fix?

☐ HER REPLY ☐ HIS REPLY   ☐ HIS REPLY ☐ HER REPLY

If you could make a wish that you could never forget, what would you wish for?

☐ HER REPLY   ☐ HIS REPLY

☐ HIS REPLY   ☐ HER REPLY

What would make you most content?

☐ HER REPLY   ☐ HIS REPLY

☐ HIS REPLY   ☐ HER REPLY

What's the worst pain you've ever felt?

☐ HER REPLY ☐ HIS REPLY

☐ HIS REPLY ☐ HER REPLY

Why do you use the word "cute"?

☐ HER REPLY ☐ HIS REPLY

☐ HIS REPLY ☐ HER REPLY

If you had to choose one thing that you could do if you were given one day to live, what would it be?

☐ HER REPLY ☐ HIS REPLY

☐ HIS REPLY ☐ HER REPLY

How would you describe the feeling of being proud?

☐ HER REPLY ☐ HIS REPLY

☐ HIS REPLY ☐ HER REPLY

Do you ever feel like you are a pawn? Why?

☐ HER REPLY ☐ HIS REPLY

☐ HIS REPLY ☐ HER REPLY

Say something about your current status.

☐ HER REPLY ☐ HIS REPLY

☐ HIS REPLY ☐ HER REPLY

What is your biggest concern about this?

☐ HER REPLY ☐ HIS REPLY   ☐ HIS REPLY ☐ HER REPLY

What would you like to see happen in the near future?

☐ HER REPLY ☐ HIS REPLY   ☐ HIS REPLY ☐ HER REPLY

If you could have one pet to share to someone, what would it be and why?

☐ HER REPLY ☐ HIS REPLY

☐ HIS REPLY ☐ HER REPLY

What is your greatest hope for the future?

☐ HER REPLY ☐ HIS REPLY

☐ HIS REPLY ☐ HER REPLY

How can you take advantage of this moment?

☐ HER REPLY ☐ HIS REPLY

☐ HIS REPLY ☐ HER REPLY

How do you make it to the end of the day?

☐ HER REPLY ☐ HIS REPLY

☐ HIS REPLY ☐ HER REPLY

What is the best advice you've ever gotten?

☐ HER REPLY ☐ HIS REPLY

☐ HIS REPLY ☐ HER REPLY

Have you ever been rejected? How did you handle it?

☐ HER REPLY ☐ HIS REPLY

☐ HIS REPLY ☐ HER REPLY

What makes you think that is important?

☐ HER REPLY ☐ HIS REPLY

____

☐ HIS REPLY ☐ HER REPLY

____

Which think-piece is your favorite?

☐ HER REPLY ☐ HIS REPLY

____

☐ HIS REPLY ☐ HER REPLY

____

What effects does watching violence have on people?

☐ HER REPLY ☐ HIS REPLY

☐ HIS REPLY ☐ HER REPLY

How would you describe the feeling of being transported back to an alien world where you are a member of a spacefaring race?

☐ HER REPLY ☐ HIS REPLY

☐ HIS REPLY ☐ HER REPLY

When was the last time you felt confident?

☐ HER REPLY ☐ HIS REPLY

☐ HIS REPLY ☐ HER REPLY

What do you do when people say things that make you want to punch them?

☐ HER REPLY ☐ HIS REPLY

☐ HIS REPLY ☐ HER REPLY

Imagine that the world was colorless. How would that make you feel?

☐ HER REPLY ☐ HIS REPLY   ☐ HIS REPLY ☐ HER REPLY

_______________________________________   _______________________________________
_______________________________________   _______________________________________
_______________________________________   _______________________________________
_______________________________________   _______________________________________
_______________________________________   _______________________________________
_______________________________________   _______________________________________
_______________________________________   _______________________________________
_______________________________________   _______________________________________
_______________________________________   _______________________________________
_______________________________________   _______________________________________

How do you deal with people around you that just let you down?

☐ HER REPLY ☐ HIS REPLY   ☐ HIS REPLY ☐ HER REPLY

_______________________________________   _______________________________________
_______________________________________   _______________________________________
_______________________________________   _______________________________________
_______________________________________   _______________________________________
_______________________________________   _______________________________________
_______________________________________   _______________________________________
_______________________________________   _______________________________________

What happens on the other side of the door?

☐ HER REPLY ☐ HIS REPLY

☐ HIS REPLY ☐ HER REPLY

What is the best advice you ever got regarding anything?

☐ HER REPLY ☐ HIS REPLY

☐ HIS REPLY ☐ HER REPLY

How important it is to you that you have friends?

□ HER REPLY □ HIS REPLY

□ HIS REPLY □ HER REPLY

What if someone gives you $100.000? What would you do with it?

□ HER REPLY □ HIS REPLY

□ HIS REPLY □ HER REPLY

What is your biggest worry?

☐ HER REPLY   ☐ HIS REPLY   ☐ HIS REPLY   ☐ HER REPLY

What is your favorite type of ice cream?

☐ HER REPLY   ☐ HIS REPLY   ☐ HIS REPLY   ☐ HER REPLY

How would you describe the feeling of being degraded?

☐ HER REPLY ☐ HIS REPLY

☐ HIS REPLY ☐ HER REPLY

What is something so important that hate? Why?

☐ HER REPLY ☐ HIS REPLY

☐ HIS REPLY ☐ HER REPLY

What has been your greatest experience?

☐ HER REPLY ☐ HIS REPLY

____
____
____
____
____
____
____
____

☐ HIS REPLY ☐ HER REPLY

____
____
____
____
____
____
____
____

What is the difference between a normal and an "abnormal" level?

☐ HER REPLY ☐ HIS REPLY

____
____
____
____
____
____
____
____

☐ HIS REPLY ☐ HER REPLY

____
____
____
____
____
____
____
____

What do you do when you're exhausted?

□ HER REPLY   □ HIS REPLY

□ HIS REPLY   □ HER REPLY

What is your favorite way to sleep?

□ HER REPLY   □ HIS REPLY

□ HIS REPLY   □ HER REPLY

Talk about the first time you had sex, or if you still haven't, talk about how you imagine it would be like.

□ HER REPLY □ HIS REPLY   □ HIS REPLY □ HER REPLY

What did you learn from your mother?

□ HER REPLY □ HIS REPLY   □ HIS REPLY □ HER REPLY

If you were to describe the color green to a blind person, how would you do it?

☐ HER REPLY ☐ HIS REPLY   ☐ HIS REPLY ☐ HER REPLY

What's so horrible about the world that you just want to let it go and go away?

☐ HER REPLY ☐ HIS REPLY   ☐ HIS REPLY ☐ HER REPLY

If you could build your dream house right away? Which house would it be?

☐ HER REPLY ☐ HIS REPLY

☐ HIS REPLY ☐ HER REPLY

What is your plan for the new season?

☐ HER REPLY ☐ HIS REPLY

☐ HIS REPLY ☐ HER REPLY

☐ HER REPLY ☐ HIS REPLY

☐ HIS REPLY ☐ HER REPLY

☐ HER REPLY ☐ HIS REPLY

☐ HIS REPLY ☐ HER REPLY

If you could be anywhere at any time, where would you want to be?

☐ HER REPLY ☐ HIS REPLY

☐ HIS REPLY ☐ HER REPLY

If you had to guess how your life story would end, how would it be?

☐ HER REPLY ☐ HIS REPLY

☐ HIS REPLY ☐ HER REPLY

If you had to choose one, which one would you most want to live without?

☐ HER REPLY ☐ HIS REPLY

☐ HIS REPLY ☐ HER REPLY

What is the most important lesson you learned in childhood?

☐ HER REPLY ☐ HIS REPLY

☐ HIS REPLY ☐ HER REPLY

What are three things you are passionate about and why?

☐ HER REPLY ☐ HIS REPLY

____
____
____
____
____
____
____

☐ HIS REPLY ☐ HER REPLY

____
____
____
____
____
____
____

What are your greatest worries?

☐ HER REPLY ☐ HIS REPLY

____
____
____
____
____
____
____

☐ HIS REPLY ☐ HER REPLY

____
____
____
____
____
____
____

What do you do to relax?

☐ HER REPLY ☐ HIS REPLY

☐ HIS REPLY ☐ HER REPLY

Why do you get an 'A+' when all of your competitors have 'B+'?

☐ HER REPLY ☐ HIS REPLY

☐ HIS REPLY ☐ HER REPLY

What do you think will be a positive outcome of the conversation?

☐ HER REPLY ☐ HIS REPLY

☐ HIS REPLY ☐ HER REPLY

What do you like about the area where you live?

☐ HER REPLY ☐ HIS REPLY

☐ HIS REPLY ☐ HER REPLY

What do you like most about yourself?

☐ HER REPLY ☐ HIS REPLY   ☐ HIS REPLY ☐ HER REPLY

Would you rather be on the bus or be on a horse?

☐ HER REPLY ☐ HIS REPLY   ☐ HIS REPLY ☐ HER REPLY

Would you rather fight or not fight?

☐ HER REPLY ☐ HIS REPLY

☐ HIS REPLY ☐ HER REPLY

What are some alternatives to keep you safe?

☐ HER REPLY ☐ HIS REPLY

☐ HIS REPLY ☐ HER REPLY

Do you have a special experience that you would like to share? Why? Why not?

☐ HER REPLY ☐ HIS REPLY

☐ HIS REPLY ☐ HER REPLY

Write about 2 songs that you love best.

☐ HER REPLY ☐ HIS REPLY

☐ HIS REPLY ☐ HER REPLY

What is the most annoying thing that has happened to you?

☐ HER REPLY ☐ HIS REPLY   ☐ HIS REPLY ☐ HER REPLY

What is the best moment of your life?

☐ HER REPLY ☐ HIS REPLY   ☐ HIS REPLY ☐ HER REPLY

Discuss how conveniences change people's lives.

☐ HER REPLY ☐ HIS REPLY

☐ HIS REPLY ☐ HER REPLY

What is the thing you're trying to change?

☐ HER REPLY ☐ HIS REPLY

☐ HIS REPLY ☐ HER REPLY

If you could be forced to be absolutely silent for 1 hour, can you do it? Why?

☐ HER REPLY ☐ HIS REPLY

☐ HIS REPLY ☐ HER REPLY

Have you ever thought about writing your last wishes? Why?

☐ HER REPLY ☐ HIS REPLY

☐ HIS REPLY ☐ HER REPLY

What was the last thing your friend said that struck you?

☐ HER REPLY ☐ HIS REPLY

☐ HIS REPLY ☐ HER REPLY

What's the favorite quote you've never heard?

☐ HER REPLY ☐ HIS REPLY

☐ HIS REPLY ☐ HER REPLY

What are the most important skills you need for the job you currently hold?

☐ HER REPLY ☐ HIS REPLY

☐ HIS REPLY ☐ HER REPLY

What are your worries being led?

☐ HER REPLY ☐ HIS REPLY

☐ HIS REPLY ☐ HER REPLY

What do you prefer, money or time? Why?

☐ HER REPLY ☐ HIS REPLY

☐ HIS REPLY ☐ HER REPLY

If you could take a single thing from an event or something that you think was inspirational, what would it be?

☐ HER REPLY ☐ HIS REPLY

☐ HIS REPLY ☐ HER REPLY

Why do you think you have to handle it so differently?

☐ HER REPLY ☐ HIS REPLY

☐ HIS REPLY ☐ HER REPLY

What's your favorite moment in college?

☐ HER REPLY ☐ HIS REPLY

☐ HIS REPLY ☐ HER REPLY

What is something you do well?

☐ HER REPLY ☐ HIS REPLY

☐ HIS REPLY ☐ HER REPLY

How would you describe the feeling of being independent?

☐ HER REPLY ☐ HIS REPLY

☐ HIS REPLY ☐ HER REPLY

List of things that are easily noted and remembered

☐ HER REPLY ☐ HIS REPLY

☐ HIS REPLY ☐ HER REPLY

Say something that will bring the world down.

☐ HER REPLY ☐ HIS REPLY

☐ HIS REPLY ☐ HER REPLY

What if you can no longer see? What would you do?

☐ HER REPLY ☐ HIS REPLY

☐ HIS REPLY ☐ HER REPLY

If you could change anything about our family, what would it be?

☐ HER REPLY ☐ HIS REPLY

☐ HIS REPLY ☐ HER REPLY

What was the best moment of your career to date?

☐ HER REPLY ☐ HIS REPLY   ☐ HIS REPLY ☐ HER REPLY

If you could only listen to one music, what would it be?

☐ HER REPLY ☐ HIS REPLY   ☐ HIS REPLY ☐ HER REPLY

List of things that I can achieve this year

☐ HER REPLY ☐ HIS REPLY

☐ HIS REPLY ☐ HER REPLY

How can you help your children cope with bullying?

☐ HER REPLY ☐ HIS REPLY

☐ HIS REPLY ☐ HER REPLY

What is the hardest thing about being a parent?

☐ HER REPLY ☐ HIS REPLY

☐ HIS REPLY ☐ HER REPLY

Do you even know how to talk about something and say what you're going to do? How?

☐ HER REPLY ☐ HIS REPLY

☐ HIS REPLY ☐ HER REPLY

Is there something that you memorized long ago and still remember? Can you write it down?

☐ HER REPLY ☐ HIS REPLY

☐ HIS REPLY ☐ HER REPLY

List the pros and cons of becoming immortal.

☐ HER REPLY ☐ HIS REPLY

☐ HIS REPLY ☐ HER REPLY

Say something that is not true about a person and have them believe it.

☐ HER REPLY ☐ HIS REPLY   ☐ HIS REPLY ☐ HER REPLY

What is something you never do?

☐ HER REPLY ☐ HIS REPLY   ☐ HIS REPLY ☐ HER REPLY

Which of your favorite songs were the best?

☐ HER REPLY ☐ HIS REPLY

☐ HIS REPLY ☐ HER REPLY

Have you ever felt like the people around you did something to you that you didn't like?

☐ HER REPLY ☐ HIS REPLY

☐ HIS REPLY ☐ HER REPLY

Does the best thing you are willing to give up for a good thing come from a certain source or does it come from nowhere?

☐ HER REPLY ☐ HIS REPLY

☐ HIS REPLY ☐ HER REPLY

When was the last time you had time to think of another option?

☐ HER REPLY ☐ HIS REPLY

☐ HIS REPLY ☐ HER REPLY

How would you react if your story appeared in the paper tomorrow?

☐ HER REPLY ☐ HIS REPLY

☐ HIS REPLY ☐ HER REPLY

What's the best way you can approach an issue?

☐ HER REPLY ☐ HIS REPLY

☐ HIS REPLY ☐ HER REPLY

If you could look at your life from the perspective of the person you are now, what would you change about your life?

☐ HER REPLY ☐ HIS REPLY

☐ HIS REPLY ☐ HER REPLY

____

What is one thing about life and why should you make a difference?

☐ HER REPLY ☐ HIS REPLY

☐ HIS REPLY ☐ HER REPLY

If you could change one thing about your life right now, what would it be?

☐ HER REPLY ☐ HIS REPLY   ☐ HIS REPLY ☐ HER REPLY

What are the top five things that irk you the most?

☐ HER REPLY ☐ HIS REPLY   ☐ HIS REPLY ☐ HER REPLY

Who is your favorite celebrity and why?

☐ HER REPLY ☐ HIS REPLY   ☐ HIS REPLY ☐ HER REPLY

What would you do to change the country and the world for the better if you were elected president?

☐ HER REPLY ☐ HIS REPLY   ☐ HIS REPLY ☐ HER REPLY

Does your love make you want to do something better? How?

□ HER REPLY □ HIS REPLY

□ HIS REPLY □ HER REPLY

If you could do whatever you wanted to right now, what would you do?

□ HER REPLY □ HIS REPLY

□ HIS REPLY □ HER REPLY

How would you describe the feeling of being tricked or even being lied to?

☐ HER REPLY ☐ HIS REPLY

☐ HIS REPLY ☐ HER REPLY

What's your favorite team to hate in fantasy?

☐ HER REPLY ☐ HIS REPLY

☐ HIS REPLY ☐ HER REPLY

What's a good story about your mother?

☐ HER REPLY ☐ HIS REPLY

☐ HIS REPLY ☐ HER REPLY

Have you ever gotten depressed while listening to music?

☐ HER REPLY ☐ HIS REPLY

☐ HIS REPLY ☐ HER REPLY